It's Saturday!
Things to Do on Your Day Off

Four Procedural Texts

by Katherine Scraper with Jayce Wolf, Madison Conner, Jeremiah Thompson, and Jaden McAdoo

Table of Contents

Focus on the Genre: Procedural Text 2
Meet the Student-Authors 4
Make Errands More Fun: Draw a Map! 6
How to Wash a Dog 8
Flipping Out with Flip Books 10
How to Make a Grilled Cheese Sandwich 12
The Writer's Craft: Procedural Text 14
Glossary 16
Make Connections Across Texts .... Inside Back Cover

Focus on the Genre

Procedural Text

What is a procedural text?

A procedural text tells how to make or do something. Examples include a recipe from a cookbook, the rules to a board game, travel directions, and learning a new math skill by following the steps in a textbook. People use procedural texts at home, in their jobs, and in their hobbies. Other names for procedural texts are technical writing, instructions, directions, or "how-tos."

What is the purpose of a procedural text?

A procedural text describes how to do something in such a way that other people can do it easily. The author clearly explains what supplies and equipment to use and what steps to follow. Some authors share tips that will help the process go more smoothly. The text usually includes one or more photographs, illustrations, or diagrams to help readers visualize, or see, how to do the steps. A picture of the finished product may be included as well.

Who is the audience for a procedural text?

Procedural texts are for everyone! People of all ages use procedural texts to learn new skills, perform science experiments, administer first aid, build, cook or bake foods, play games, create crafts, or improve their abilities in music or sports. People can find procedural texts in books, magazines, newspapers, pamphlets, instructions that come with purchases, and on the Internet.

Features of a Procedural Text

- The title clearly identifies the topic.
- The author includes photographs, illustrations, or diagrams to help explain the process.
- The introduction tells why the reader will want to make or do the activity or project.
- Most sentences begin with verbs. The sentences are short and direct.
- Supplies and equipment are listed in the order in which they are used.
- The directions are given as numbered steps or short paragraphs with sequence words.

How do you read a procedural text?

The title will tell you what you can learn to make or do. Next, check the list of supplies and equipment to see if you have everything you need. After that, read through all of the steps and study the pictures to make sure you understand what to do. Then begin! As you work, pay special attention to any tips the author provides.

Meet the Student-Authors

"Make Errands More Fun: Draw a Map!"
by Jayce Wolf

"My family runs lots of errands on Saturdays. Instead of just riding along, I draw maps of where we're going. Try it . . . it's fun!"

"How to Wash a Dog"
by Madison Conner

"Do you have to do chores on Saturdays? I do! One of my jobs is washing the dog. I'll teach you how!"

▲ Jayce, Madison, Jeremiah, and Jaden attend Lincoln Elementary School in El Dorado, Kansas.

"Flipping Out with Flip Books"
by Jeremiah Thompson

"By Saturday afternoon, I sometimes am bored. Then it's time to make a flip book. You can choose any subject you like."

"How to Make a Grilled Cheese Sandwich"
by Jaden McAdoo

"Sometimes I make my own lunch on Saturdays. My parents don't want me to use the stove, but I can make a great grilled cheese sandwich using a toaster and microwave!"

Tools Writers Use

Text and Graphic Features

Authors of procedural texts include text and graphic features to support their ideas and help readers understand what they are saying. Text features, such as headings, subheadings, bulleted lists, captions, and special fonts, help readers locate information, because they look different from the main text. Graphic features, such as illustrations, photographs, and diagrams, help readers interpret, or figure out, the meaning of the text. That way, readers can be more successful in completing the procedural activity or project.

Make Errands More Fun: Draw a Map!

The next time you run errands with your family, take along a drawing pad and pencil to create a map of your route. Here's how:

1. Write down your starting location. Note the direction you are traveling in. Some cars have a compass on the control panel. Or you can use a pocket compass.

2. Make notes or sketches of any landmarks you pass. Landmarks could be a **store**, park, office building, or school.

3. Each time you turn, write down the new direction. Note the name of the new street or road. **Keep** drawing or writing about landmarks you pass.

4. When you get to where you are going, write down your location.

5. When you get home, use your notes and sketches to draw a map. Label the streets or roads. Put in landmarks if you can.

Collect your maps in a folder. When you have several, put them together to make a map of your community!

✱ **TIP: Be sure the top of your map is north, the bottom is south, the left side is west, and the right side is east. Include the compass points off to one side.**

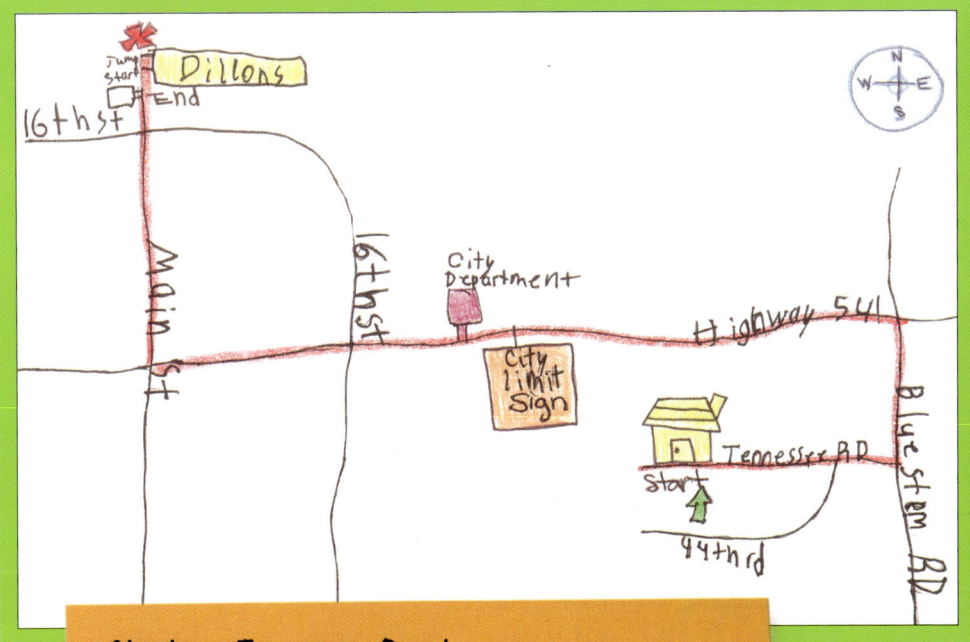

- Start on Tennessee Road.
- Drive east toward Bluestem Road.
- Turn left (north) on Bluestem Road.
- Turn left (west) on Highway 541.
- Follow Highway 541 until you get to Main Street. You will pass the City Limit sign and the City Department building.
- Make a right on Main Street (driving north) until you pass 16th Street. The grocery store (Dillons) is on your right.

7

How to Wash a Dog

Things You'll Need:
- tub of water
- brush
- shampoo
- conditioner
- towel
- dog treat

Step 1: Get the water at the **right** temperature. It should not be too hot or too cold.

Step 2: **Brush** your dog. Then put the dog in the tub.

Step 3: Put shampoo on the dog. Rub it gently all over the dog's fur. Be careful! Don't get shampoo in your dog's eyes!

Step 4: Rinse off the shampoo.

Step 5: Repeat Steps 3 and 4 with conditioner.

Step 6: **Wrap** the dog in the towel.

Step 7: Give your dog a treat!

* TIP: Some dogs are afraid of baths, so speak gently to your pet!

Reread the Informational Texts

Analyze the Texts
- What are the parts of each procedural text?
- The second author lists needed supplies and equipment. How did she decide what to list first? Second? Last?
- What sequence words do the authors use?

Analyze the Tools Writers Use: Text and Graphic Features

Look at the directions for drawing a map.
- What does the title tell you about this text?
- How does the tip help you?

Look at the directions for washing a dog.
- What subheading does the author use? Why?
- How does the graphic feature (illustration) help you understand the text?

Focus on Words: Multiple-Meaning Words

Words that look and sound the same can have different meanings. They can even be different parts of speech. Make a chart like the one below. Find each word in the text. Use context clues to help you figure out the word's meaning and part of speech. Then use a dictionary to find another meaning for the word. Record the part of speech.

Page	Word	Meaning #1 from Context	Part of Speech	Meaning #2 from Dictionary	Part of Speech
6	store				
6	keep				
8	right				
8	brush				
8	wrap				

> The author clearly states his topic in the title. He gives his work a fun title to get readers' attention.

Flipping Out with Flip Books

Try this fun project anytime, anywhere. All you need is a pad of sticky notes (or a small, unlined notebook), a pencil, crayons or markers, and your imagination!

> The author uses numbered steps to clearly show readers what to do.

Step 1: Draw a **cover** for your flip book on the first sticky note. Include a title.

Step 2: Draw a simple picture on the second sticky note. The picture should show something that can move. It could be a person jumping, an animal running, a flower growing, or a car moving down the street.

Step 3: Draw the same picture on the third sticky note, but make one small **change** that starts to show the movement.

Step 4: Draw the same picture on the fourth sticky note. Make another small change that shows the next movement.

> The author begins each sentence with a verb to keep the steps short and direct.

Step 5: Continue drawing a new picture on each sticky note until the movement is completed.

Step 6: Color the pictures.

Step 7: Hold the edge of the pad in one hand and **flip** the pages with your other hand. The figure will appear to move right before your eyes! Now, share your "movie" with your family and friends.

> A series of illustrations helps readers visualize important steps in the process.

✱ TIP: Draw your picture close to the outer edge of each sticky note so you can see it easily when you flip the pages.

How to Make a Grilled Cheese Sandwich

The author gives a brief introduction to interest readers in the topic.

Try this recipe for a quick, tasty, and nutritious lunch.

Supplies:

The bulleted list shows readers what supplies they will need and in what order they will use them.

- 2 slices of bread
- toaster
- small plate
- butter knife
- butter
- 1 slice of cheese
- microwave

How to Make It:
First, put the bread in the toaster. When it pops up, put it on the **plate**. Next, use the butter knife to **spread** butter on one side of each slice. After that, put the cheese between the sides of the bread with no butter. Finally, put the sandwich in the microwave for fifteen seconds. Ding! It's done!

The author includes a tip to add to readers' enjoyment and convenience when doing the project.

❋ **TIP:** To make a complete meal, add some carrot sticks, an apple, and a glass of milk.

Reread the Informational Texts

Analyze the Texts
- What is the purpose of these two procedural texts?
- How are the introductions alike? How are they different?
- One author writes directions in a paragraph with sequence words. The other author uses numbered steps. Which set of directions do you like better? Why?
- Why does the first author say you need to use your imagination?

Analyze the Tools Writers Use: Text and Graphic Features

Look at the directions for making flip books.
- How do pictured steps help you understand the text?
- How does the caption help you understand the text?

Look at the directions for making a grilled cheese sandwich.
- Look at the list of ingredients. How do the bullets help you?
- Why is the word "tip" in capital letters?

Focus on Words: Multiple-Meaning Words

Make a chart like the one below. Find each word in the text. Use context clues to help you figure out the word's meaning and part of speech. Then use a dictionary to find another meaning for the word. Record the part of speech.

Page	Word	Meaning #1 from Context	Part of Speech	Meaning #2 from Dictionary	Part of Speech
10	cover				
11	change				
11	flip				
12	plate				
12	spread				

The Writer's Craft

How does an author write a
Procedural Text?

Reread "Flipping Out with Flip Books" and think about what the author did to write this procedural text. How did he explain his project in a way that readers could understand? How can you, as a writer, develop your own procedural text?

1. Decide on an Activity or Project

Remember, a procedural text describes something the author knows how to do well. In this text, the author wants to tell readers how to make a project he enjoys—a flip book. He includes a brief introduction explaining why readers may want to do this activity.

2. Decide What Supplies and Equipment to Use

If your activity needs supplies or equipment, create a bulleted list. List each item in the order readers will use it.

3. Decide What Steps to Use

You can write using numbered steps or short paragraphs with sequencing words. Begin sentences with verbs, and use short, direct sentences. Ask yourself:

- Which method—numbered steps or short paragraphs—will be clearer to my audience?
- If I use numbered steps, how will I order them?
- If I use paragraphs, how will I divide them? What sequencing words will I use to make my steps logical?
- Do I need to include any tips to help readers be successful? If so, where should I put them?

4. Decide What Art to Use

Pictures help readers visualize how to do the activity and show what the finished product looks like. Ask yourself:

- What photographs could I take as I go through the steps? What photographs could someone take of me working?
- What illustrations would help readers understand the steps?
- What diagrams could I use to explain one or more steps?
- What art could I add as I go? What art could I put at the end?
- What captions or labels could I add to my art?

5. Field-Test Your Writing

Ask a friend to read and try your activity. Write down anything that confuses your friend or any questions he or she asks. Use this information to add needed supplies, equipment, steps, tips, or art to your procedural writing.

Activity or Project	making a flip book
Things I Need	pad of sticky notes, pencil, crayons or markers, imagination
Steps	make cover, draw pages, flip pages
Art	illustrations of steps

Glossary

brush   *verb* (BRUSH) apply a brush to; touch gently against (page 8)

change   *noun* (CHANJE) modification or alteration (page 11)

cover   *noun* (KUH-ver) top or front part of a book or magazine (page 10)

flip   *verb* (FLIP) turn over quickly (page 11)

keep   *verb* (KEEP) continue doing something (page 6)

plate   *noun* (PLATE) a dish, usually round, on which food is served (page 12)

right   *adjective* (RITE) correct; proper; appropriate (page 8)

spread   *verb* (SPRED) apply evenly to a surface (page 12)

store   *noun* (STOR) a place where items are sold (page 6)

wrap   *verb* (RAP) cover by winding around something (page 8)